"Oh my beloved! Now what if I say,
Your soul is the chorus to the song of my soul."

TANISHKA TYAGI

NewDelhi • London

BLUEROSE PUBLISHERS
India | U.K.

Copyright © Tanishka Tyagi 2024

All rights reserved by author. No part of this publication may be reproduced, stored in a retrieval system or transmitted in any form or by any means, electronic, mechanical, photocopying, recording or otherwise, without the prior permission of the author. Although every precaution has been taken to verify the accuracy of the information contained herein, the publisher assume no responsibility for any errors or omissions. No liability is assumed for damages that may result from the use of information contained within.

BlueRose Publishers takes no responsibility for any damages, losses, or liabilities that may arise from the use or misuse of the information, products, or services provided in this publication.

For permissions requests or inquiries regarding this publication, please contact:

BLUEROSE PUBLISHERS
www.BlueRoseONE.com
info@bluerosepublishers.com
+91 8882 898 898
+4407342408967

ISBN: 978-93-5989-420-1

Cover design: Tanishka Tyagi (Author), Suruchi
Typesetting: Tanishka Tyagi (Author), Namrata Saini
Illustrations: Tanishka Tyagi (Author), Rawpixel and Pinterest

First Edition: July 2024

Introduction

As you open this book, you are invited on a poetic journey through the soul of a young poet, her words flow like a river, weaving tales of love, passion, and emotion. With each verse you'll find yourself lost in a world full of ecstasy , longing, and raw honesty.

Allow me to introduce you to the mesmerising world of Tanishka Tyagi, a talented poet who has been creating magic with words since the tender age of 12. At just 17, this young artist has poured their heart and soul onto the pages of this book, inviting you on a journey through the core of her soul. Tanishka has mastered the art of painting emotions with words, With each verse you are reminded of the transformative power of a cosmic love and the depths of human connections.

Tanishka Tyagi's collection of poems is a sublime exploration of the complexities of love, a heartfelt journey through the landscape of human emotions. In this rich tapestry of verses, the poet weaves a narrative that resonates with readers on a profound level, delving into the intricate nuances of a cosmic love.

The collection opens with a poignant piece that sets the tone for what follows a passionate and introspective exploration of love in its myriad forms. Tyagi's poetic voice is unmistakably sincere, inviting readers into a world where emotions are laid bare, unfiltered and raw. The authenticity of the emotions portrayed is perhaps one of the collection's most compelling features.

The thematic depth of the collection is evident in the recurring motifs that thread through the poems. The moon and stars emerge as symbols, recurring elements that tie the collection together. These celestial symbols, often associated with timeless and boundless love, are skilfully used to convey the idea that love transcends the limitations of time and space. It adds a layer of universality to the poems, making them relatable to readers across diverse experiences.

One of the strengths of Tyagi's collection lies in the varied perspectives on love that it presents. Each poem offers a unique lens through which the poet examines different facets of love-sometimes as an intoxicating elixir, at other times as a bittersweet longing. This diversity prevents the collection from becoming monotonous, offering readers a rich and multifaceted exploration of the central theme.

While the collection predominantly explores the theme of cosmic love, there are moments of introspection that touch upon the broader canvas of human emotions. Tyagi delves into the intricacies of the human psyche, exploring themes of self-discovery and vulnerability. These moments of introspection add depth to the collection, elevating it beyond a simple exploration of romantic theme. .

A notable aspect of Tyagi's poetry is the optimistic undercurrent that runs through many of the poems. Despite the inevitable challenges and heartaches that love brings, there's a persistent hopefulness and belief that love has the power to endure. The recurring motif of the moon, a steadfast presence in the night sky, becomes a symbol of this enduring hope. It's a refreshing perspective that distinguishes the collection from more somber portrayals of love.

As much as the Team and the Author is excited for the readers to delve into this masterpiece, we hope the readers are equally awaiting and eager. Be prepared for your heart to swell and your soul to dance as you embark on a journey through Tanishka's soul of poetic expression.

Playlist.

J's lullaby (Darling I'd wait for you)	Delaney Bailey
Ode to Vivian	Patrick Watson
Je te laisserai des mots	Patrick Watson
Mystery of love	Sufjan Stevens
Silence	Two lanes
Rue des trois frères	Fabrizio Paterlini
In between	J.J Pfeifer, Grace Meredith
You're mine, You!	Chet Baker
Ferme Les Yeux	Sylvain Chauveau
I wanted to leave	SYML
Wind song	Ludovico Einaudi
Dream river	Woodsman
The wisp sings	Winter Aid
Before you left	Yehezkel Raz
Over the moon	The Marías
Let's fall in love	Ella Fitzgerald
Loving you	Elvis Presley
Everything	The black shirt
Only	RYX
Love letters from the sea to the shore	Delaney Bailey
Where's my love (Acoustic)	SYML
Lights are on	Tom Rosenthal
Euphor	Novo Amor, Lowswimmer
Come into my arms	November ultra

Tanishka Tyagi

One Soul

On Love	Delaney Bailey
And I love you so	Perry Como
Fade into you	Mazzy star
Closer	Nuages
With you	Jimin, Ha Sung Woon

Tanishka Tyagi

One Soul

This book, my love
This book is a reflection of you.
Everything I wrote
Is everything I saw in you.
Read it as if you're looking
Into your soul, through mine.
Read it like
You've never loved yourself enough,
And love yourself the most for a while.
Read it with a smile ,
And with a thought that
All your soul was poured
On paper of 'One Soul'.
Read it with a mind that says,
You deserve it,
You deserve it all.

Tanishka Tyagi

One Soul

You have the stars in your eyes
When you look at me,
I feel the *galaxy* within me forming.
You have the *peace in your voice*
When you call my name,
I feel my soul's unknown wounds *healing.*
You have the *world in your arms*
When you embrace me,
I feel our universe eventually
Colliding.

You and I,
In my land of nod.
When my eyes are closed,
And mind wide awake.

Tanishka Tyagi

One Soul

Let the time freeze
When we're together.
Let the souls heal
When we're together.
Let the eyes feel
When we're together.
Let us be us
When we're together.
Let the waves of the ocean subside
When we're together.
Let the Moon shine on its own
When we're together.
Let the Sun feel cold
When we're together.
Let everything impossible, transpire
When we're together.
Let the world know.
That we're together.
Let the world know
That–
That we're together.

~ Togetherness mustn't be mistaken by presence.
For, you may be present but not necessarily be one,
Thus, the intimacy of souls, mustn't be mistaken
By the intimacy of bodies.

Tanishka Tyagi

One Soul

O my beloved,
now what if I say
Your soul is the *chorus,*
To the *song* of my soul.

Tanishka Tyagi

One Soul

I, my love;
I found my true colours in your shadow,
The colours that were yours are now mine,
For you never had a shadow
My love,
You always had a rainbow
That only I could see.

One Soul

If I merely had *thirteen* minutes left to life,
And I were to express my love for you,
I wouldn't make a sound,
I wouldn't utter a word,
I wouldn't confess.
Rather I would just look at you,
Deep into those crescent-like eyes.
Keep myself quiet
And *let the silence around us,*
Echo the love I have for you.
Let the moment around us
Capture the way I look at you,
Let the moment capture
An eternity.
And Oh! what a beautiful ending it will be,
 to my soul
Which since will forever live in your soul.

~ With this, we let the
Moment of silence
Capture the sound of an eternity.

One Soul

Oh! those eyes,
Your eyes divulge
A divergent story every day,
Each story talks about love.

Oh! my soul,
Take a glance at my crazy soul,
My soul is a listener,
Perpetually, enormously, inevitably
My soul,
My soul fall for yours.

~ How innocently wise to have made
The right choice.

One Soul

Even if the darkness surrounds me
I'll still spot your shadow.

One Soul

Darling, do you know?
The Sun shines brighter
When it's rays fall at you.
The Moon takes the light
When gazes into your eyes.
Do you know?
The stars, they twinkle
For they can't bear your beauty.
I hope you know,
The universe is just a reflection of you,
Mon chéri.

~ The universe,
Is *just* a reflection of you.

10:20 am

"The universe is just
a reflection of you

Mon chéri"

One Soul

You and me,
Me and you,
We go beyond distance,
I'll travel the universe to be with you.
You and me,
Me and you,
We go beyond language,
I'll learn the language of love
Only for you.
You and me,
Me and you,
We go beyond everything,
For, its you;
You are my everything.
And thus,
"Everything" seems like "nothing"
When I look at you.
You and me,
Me and you,
We're a divine connection,
Made of stars,
To shine brighter
Then who we are
When we are "we"
And not "You and me".

Tanishka Tyagi

One Soul

You look at the universe
And the universe looks at you,
You say "You're beautiful"
And it says "You're too"....

It says to the stars and the Moon,
Look I found someone
"Shining brighter than you,"
I looked into his eyes,
And the fact he said I am beautiful
Makes me groove.
I can't believe he calls me beautiful,
When he's just as beautiful as
Infinites of me.
Does he even know?
He's looking into a mirror and not the sky?
Does he know ,
I am just a reflection
Of his cosmic eyes?
I need to tell him,
Tell him that,
My beauty pales in comparison to his charm.
So the next time he looks at me
I'll be the first to say,
"You're so beautiful
Maybe I want to be like you,
My little star."
Oh! but the beauty of the star
Pales in comparison to his charm.
Maybe I just wish to be like him.
Him as in who he is, just how he is.
Exactly like that. He's perfect.

Tanishka Tyagi

One Soul

So darling,
The next time you look at the universe,
Be ready to hear, what might seem surreal,
My love, it will tell you what you actually are.

One Soul

Even so, you're a rose
With thorns,
I'll always hold you
In my soul.
Despite the spikes
you have in you,
I'll always be with you,
For those thorns you carry;
Make me strong,
With every touch
Of your petal,
I feel your love.
Thus, even so you're a rose
With thorns,
I'll always hold you
In my soul.

One Soul

On one starry night,
I'll look into your eyes,
For my brightest star
In my star's eyes.

And then I'll say
I love you,
Consider my love
Like I'll bring down the stars
For you,
My star boy, you are,
Say back "Yes I am a star."
I'll say "Yes you are"
While my eyes still be looking
Into yours.
And gazing the constellation
Named love forming in your eyes.
With all the heart I pour
Into my star's eyes.

On one starry night,
I'll look into your eyes,
For my brightest star
In my star's eyes.

Tanishka Tyagi

One Soul

I love you so much that
If I tell the Sun,
It would release all the fire within
And turn into an ice cube.
I love you so much that
If I tell the stars,
They would stop twinkling
And burst into tears becoming meteors.
I love you so much that
If I tell the Moon,
It will start to shine on its own.
I love you so much that
If I tell the sky,
It will bend down on its knees.

Tanishka Tyagi

One Soul

I love, love;
For, Love is an art,
Love is a song,
Love is a poem,
Love is the Galaxy,
Love is the Moon,
Love is a feeling,
Love is a healing,
Love is a teaching,
Love is everything
That has no bounds,
Love is everything
That cannot be defined,
Love loves you,

Love is you.

Tanishka Tyagi

One Soul

Everything makes sense
When you're in love.
You feel the love
In the smallest things on Earth,
You feel the emotions
In this monotonous world of war,
You feel the hope
On the darkest roads of life.
You feel the smile
On the face of a flower.
Everything makes sense
When you're in love.
For the earth is made for lovers,
And If it's love, it's meant to
Make sense.

One Soul

I picked up a rose today.
Couple of foldings in her soul
I tried to unfold,
Witnessed in a while,
She's all empty from inside,
Each petal out and she was only all about things
That'll fade with time.
A withered rose,
Seems pretty until she's bright, right?
But what about a withered soul?
Would you tear that too,
Would you throw that too
When it's not as pretty as it used to?

So it's what you did to me,
Picked up my soul from the ashes,
Unfolded the layers of my core
Even I didn't care about,
Perhaps, didn't even know about,
Shook in a way I want to know
How did you know
I had so much in me?
But so is not what you did to me,
You didn't abandon me, a withered soul.
You didn't tear the petals of my soul,
You didn't throw me away, you kept me,
Like a rose in a vintage diary of French love quotes,
Not for aesthetics but for memories, for love & hope.
To keep it forever.
You didn't throw me away,
When I wasn't how I was supposed to be,
When I wasn't as "pretty" as I used to be.
You still made me realize
How I was a portray of times that made me fade away,
How I was still breathing along with life
As a proof to my willed up strength, each day.

Tanishka Tyagi

One Soul

Now that you believe I'll thrive,
So for you, I will.
I'll be the flower all flourished,
A soul, once withered
Is flourishing as each day goes by,
Since for the first time,
Someone came and didn't just pass by,
Someone came and paid attention to the,
Beauty of the dead flower, and wilt petals.
Someone cared about the petals and stems,
Holding onto they're bare soul,
Pleading for themselves to not be thrown,
Just since now, they're not as "pretty" as they used to be.
The courage they had, the petals and stems,
Were hard to be shown.
Someone, being you, taught me to bloom,
To live and love and hope.
Someone being you
Made me alive,
When all my inhales exhales
Seemed nothing but futile.

So for "someone", being you,
I'll thrive and flourish, out of a withered soul.
So for "someone", being you,
I'll become the "someone", you deserve.

Tanishka Tyagi

One Soul

I fear my soul,
I fear my mind,
I fear my heart,
What if one day
It doesn't loves you
Anymore?
It doesn't thinks of you
Anymore?
It doesn't feels you
Anymore?
In that case,
I wouldn't have a life
And a reason to live.
Hence,
I would tear apart my whole self,
Tear apart my soul,
My mind and my heart.
For it makes no sense,
To be alive and breathe
In a life that has no means.

One Soul

Something about your smile these days
Makes me want to believe,
You are happy from the soul,
I could see it all;
The genuine pure smile you carry,
It makes me want to believe,
Your soul is healing,
I know you too would love
Seeing your beloved being happy,
Just like me when I see you
Laughing, cracking and joking.

Oh! I know how hard it has been for you,
You've come across many hardships,
Ups and downs as high as a mount
And I am proud of you,
Cause look at you now;
Stronger, powerful, much more confident and talented.
This is how it was always meant to be,
For you to be stronger,
You had to surpass the strong.
For you to be who you are right now,
You had to face all those times you've spent alone.
For you to be alive right here in the present,
You had to fight all night long.
I am proud of you and every part of you.
You were always right,
And you always will be.
Your journey has been unfathomably inspiring,
Looking at you how you became a
Galaxy from a star,
Rose from a petal,
Flower from a bud,
Rainbow from colors,

Tanishka Tyagi

One Soul

Ocean from a drop,
I say I am proud of you,
Beyond my soul and heart.

So now I hope this smile of yours;
To never fade away like the clouds in the sky,
Rather be the sky,
That'd always be alive,
In every consequence of life.

Tanishka Tyagi

One Soul

You fall,
You stand up,
You continue,
It's okay, that's life.
That's what makes life, a life.
However, when it comes to falling.
I'd never want to see you falling,
And I wish you never do.
Nevertheless, when it comes to *falling*
I'd love to see you *fall*
and I hope you do.

~ Fall in love.
Falling in love is like
Falling into a deep river of
Boundless distinct emotions,
Leading to your destination,
The ocean of love.
It's like falling into a hollow land of rock
And filling it with love, hope and life,
So even the rock can feel alive.
Trust me, fall in love,
A love kinda love,
Not the clichéd love.
The forever eternal,
Inevitably enlivening love.
For once you do,
I promise,
You wouldn't want to stand up,
You'd want to stay;
Stay there forever,
You'd want to stay fallen forever.

bloom with grace

Let's fall in *love*

Beautiful   & well minded

One Soul

I wanna be nothing
But someone you could tell your heart to,
Someone you could talk all night to,
Someone who makes you feel happy,
Soulful, profound and free,
Someone who gives you a shoulder to rely on,
While the tears drop from those ocean eyes,
Someone who makes you feel optimistic
When u feel low,
Someone who gives you a motive
To keep trying and never give up,
Someone who could love you
The way you love the world with all your
Heart and gratitude,
I could just keep writing about what I want to be, to you....
But In the end, I only want to be,
Someone that could just be yours.
This is all I want to be,
And I think…
This is all I am meant to be.

One Soul

And when we meet,
I hope u listen to the silence,
It'll speak,
It'll speak a billion emotions,
I hope u feel all of that.

And when we meet,
I hope u don't wipe off my tears,
It'll flow,
It'll flow like a river,
For it has waited beyond
An ocean for those pacific eyes.

And when we meet,
I just hope you live in me,
In my silence, in my eyes,
In that moment, where our souls tie.
Let's live together,
Forever, in that moment
Of our union.

One Soul

And even if
We're together in this life,
I feel like one lifetime
Isn't enough to be with you.
To love you and to make you realize
How precious you are, to my soul.
I wanna be with you,
Until the Sun stops rising,
Until the birds stop chirping,
Until the waves stop hitting the shore,
Until the world stops breathing,
I wanna be with you
Until the universe apocalypse.

Tanishka Tyagi

7:24pm

I want to be with you my darling
I want to be with you
Until the universe apocalypse

One Soul

I love star gazing,
I'd look at you for hours,
You're the only star in my sky,
The only star my Earth revolves around,
So when I say I love star gazing,
I mean, I love looking at you,
Looking like a star,
My only star.

One Soul

You seem like love, something inexpressible,
Lovely, a feeling, a lovely feeling.
You feel like love, something inexpressible,
Lovely, a feeling, a lovely feeling.
Oh! You are love, a thing so inexpressible,
Loveliest, a feeling, the most lovely lively feeling.

Tanishka Tyagi

Made with love|

One Soul

When I look at you,
I see poetries.
I see museum of a soul.
I see things that you don't show,
I see your deepest scars and
Your brightest loss,
It's so bright, you squint your eyes,
It's so bright, it always catches my sight.
When I look at you
I see things that you don't show,
But I am glad,
You've finally gained enough strength
That you don't squint no more,
You face, you face yourself,
You face the circumstance,
You face the world and your inner self.
You understand your soul,
Heal your wounds,
And don't forget to
Love yourself too.
When I look at you,
I see poetries.
I see museum of a soul.
I see the strongest one,
I see the one;
Who won my heart, mind, soul,
Every ounce of my whole.

Tanishka Tyagi

One Soul

I find myself intellectual
Until I look into your eyes,
And then I find myself,
Caught in your soul
Just like a fool.

~ This, my love
Is the only grip,
I wish would never be released,
And the only way
I wish to be fooled.

One Soul

Need no Hennessy ,
For zilch is as intoxicating
As you, your soul and those
Brown Jupiter eyes.
It's the moment of my gaze into you,
I find myself under the influence
Of a constellation of stars named, you.
Do not handle over the corpse reviver,
For I want to be blind drunk on you,
Until I've lost the consciousness
Of being unconscious.
And remind myself,
It was me who lost myself in you,
While you were still looking at me
With those brown Jupiter like captivating eyes.
Need no Hennessy,
For zilch is as intoxicating
as you.

One Soul

When I look at you,
I smile,
I smile fondly,
I smile unknowingly,
I smile like a crazy,
I smile.
I smile as if I've never smiled before,
I smile the way I've never smiled before,
I smile like I see heaven
And indeed, I do.
I smile.
Above all, a smile that shines
From a glimpse of you,
Is not just a smile,
It's a drop of the ocean,
In my eyes for you,
My love, it's my love for you
That overflows my eyes,
And slides down to the lips,
Making them shine,
Making my soul smile.
I smile,
I smile fondly,
I smile unknowingly,
I smile like crazy.
When I look at you
I smile.

Notes

One Soul

The encounter to these two roads
Is driving me crazy.
What shall I do ?
Have Faith? Believe?
Since everything will be
As it's meant to be?
For here after,
My eyes are laid on two path ways,
Puzzled mind quandarying upon the paths.
Sight of ways, one that leads to you or
Perhaps, a way that leads to incessant.
One being the wait, being worth,
With you in the end,
All my faith paying off.
One being the "wait" to its "present participle,"
Waiting and waiting and waiting all alone,
Now being with you seems futile,
As if all my faith was just for faith all this time.

Nonetheless , I'll wait,
I'll wait all my life, for you.
For the hope of you,
Is the hope to life.

~ Therefore,
Hoping we encounter on
each other's way
to make *our* way out.

Tanishka Tyagi

One Soul

If you ever fall in love
with someone else,
I'll remember there's always
A Moon in the sky,
We don't look for
In light,
But crave for
at night.

Tanishka Tyagi

One Soul

"Nothing lasts forever"
They said,
"Forever isn't a thing,"
"Nothing lasts forever,"
Why is it not?
Who said it is not?
Forever is eternity,
And eternal is my love for you,
Eternity binds us into one soul.
Therefore, we'll tell them,
I'll tell them,
Forever is a thing,
We'll show them.
Until we are,
forever is.

For once, let's consider as if ,
"Nothing lasts forever,"
And so will I pragmatically,
But my love for you?
My love for you,
will always remain in the universe,
Like the stars when scattered.
Hence, even this way,
Forever is a thing.
We'll show them,
Until our love is,
Forever is.

Tanishka Tyagi

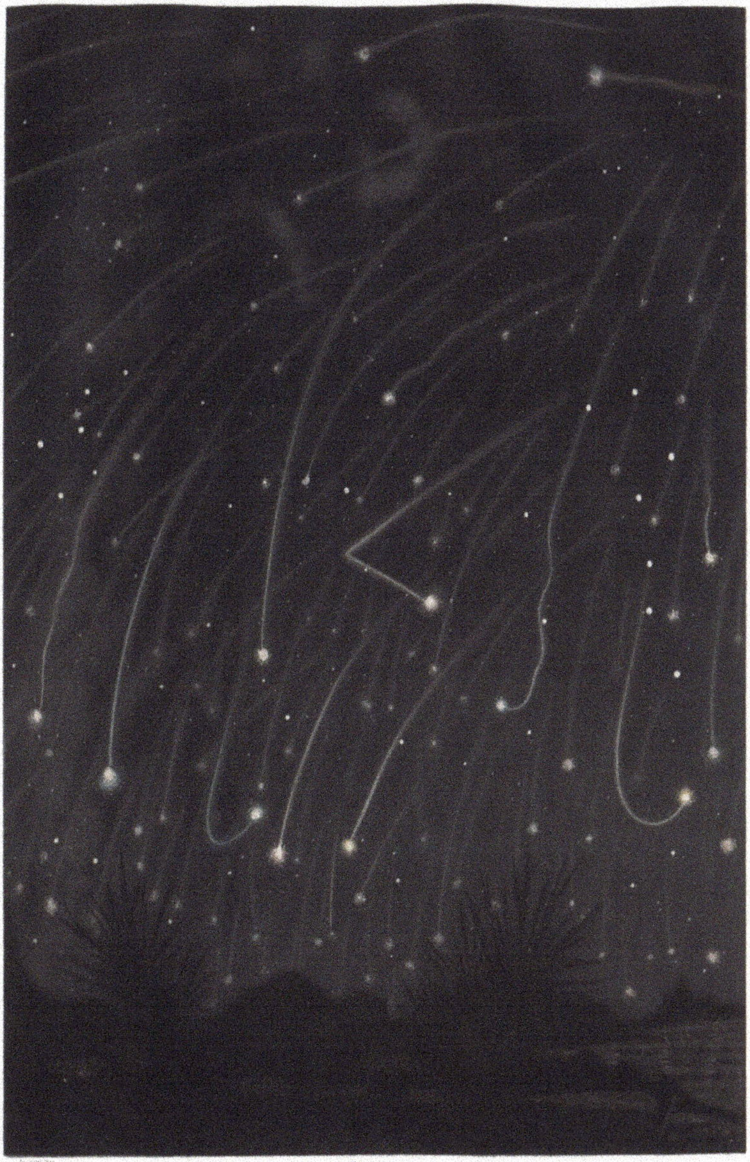

THE NOVEMBER METEORS.

As observed between Midnight and 5 o'clock A.M. on the Night of November 13-14, 1868.

One Soul

Your eyes scintillating.
Lips as the pink tourmaline.
Moles as the abalone pearls.
Clavicle looks as the constellations.
Eyes as unfathomable as the ocean.
Nose as flawless as Matterhorn.
Exquisitely created as Adonis.
Immortal as the Aphrodite.
An effervescent seraphic soul.

-All this being for the words,
Nothing competes your allure,
My love.

Tanishka Tyagi

1:36 am

My dearest

Your eyes scintillating
Lips as the pink tourmaline
Moles as the abalone pearls
Clavicle looks as the constellations
Eyes as unfathomable as the ocean
Nose as flawless as Matterhorn
Exquisitely created as Adonis
Immortal as the Aphrodite
An effervescent seraphic soul

-All this being for the words
Nothing competes your allure
My love

One Soul

When the world is…

When the world's quiet,
I'll recite my poem in your ears,
I'll whisper each word aloud,
The words so,
will echo in your soul forevermore.

When the world's in turmoil,
I'll write poems for you, in peace.
For, calm reside inside you,
No turmoil ever, is greater than the
Tranquility of your soul forevermore.

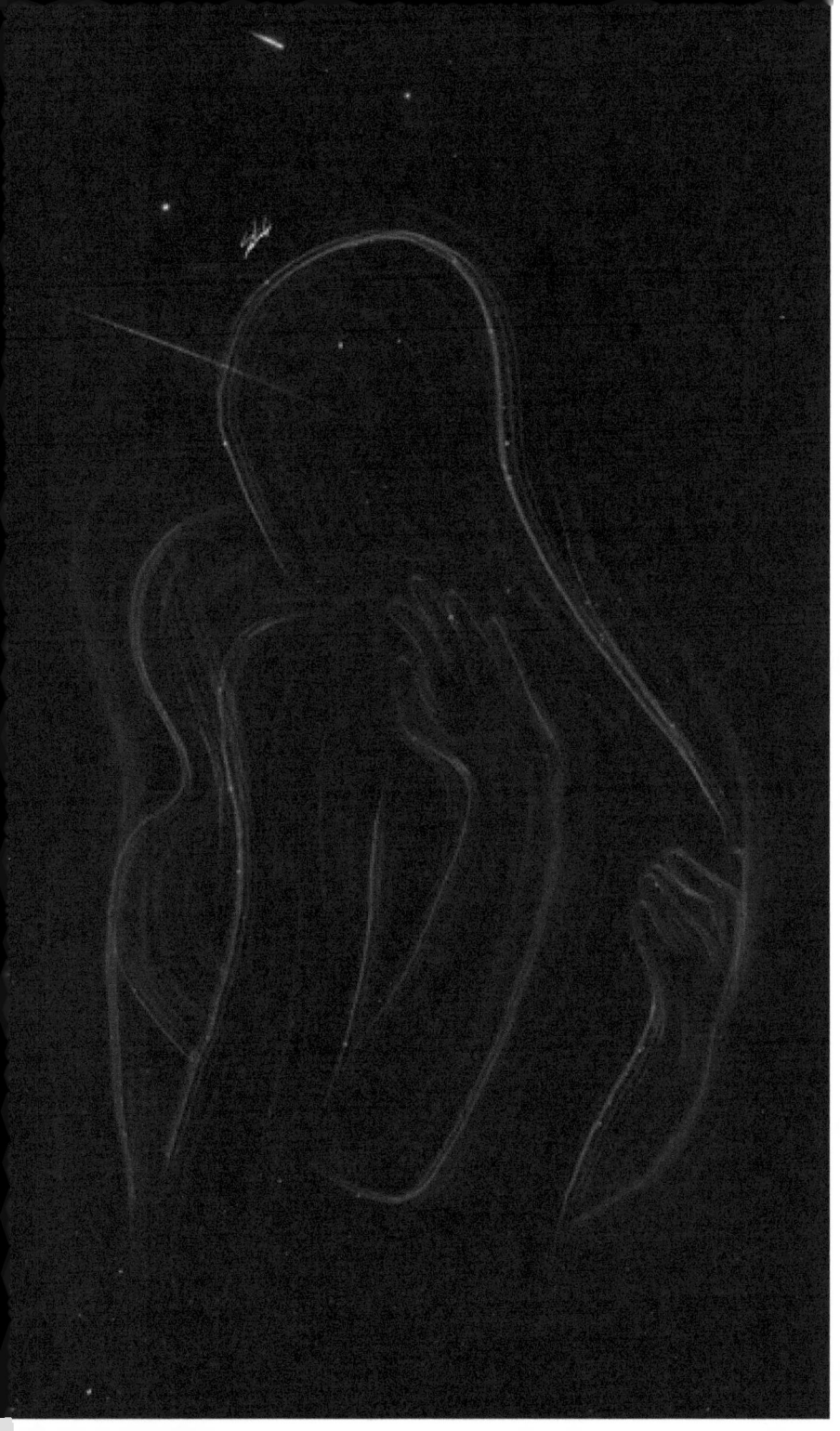

One Soul

Since I found you,
I watch the flowers bloom,
On a blue Moon's night.
Since I found you,
I feel the snowfall
In mid-July,
You gave me an eye full of
Love and life.
Since I found you,
Everything seems like,
A warm spring noon time.

Tanishka Tyagi

One Soul

Hold my hand,
Let's dance together
To the music,
Life is playing.
Sometimes it plays
A cheerful one,
And sometimes a gloomy,
But if we're together,
There's nothing to worry,
So come,
Hold my hand,
Let's dance to the music,
Life's playing.

Tanishka Tyagi

Everything about love is you,
Everything about you is love.
They say "love is blind",
For all a lover sees in love, is love.
Everywhere there's love,
In everything, there's love.
Therefore ,
I love, love
I love feeling love,
I love being in love.

They say "love is blind",
Love isn't blind.
I don't believe in this cliché,
People are,
People are blind.
Love is all about seeing the flaws,
And still being able to love.
Love isn't blind,
It's about making each other better being,
Since nobody is born perfect.
Love isn't blind,
Love is about giving each other
Eyes full of love and kind,
So if love seems blind to you,
I am sorry but,
It's not love, honey.
For love is never blind,
The people are.

One Soul

O my beloved,
I'll never get tired of
Writing letters to you,
Even if I wish to write one from my grave,
I merrily would.
Since, all of my reason to feel alive
Is you. Wherefore,
It's you, the one
That could keep me alive
Even in my grave,
Is you.

If souls could always dwell above,
  Thou ne'er had'st left thy sphere;
Or could we keep the souls we love,
  I ne'er should lose thee here.

One Soul

My dearest,
I don't want you to do
Anything for me,
I just want you to let me do
Everything for you,
I would bring the colours of rainbow
And paint your life like a beautiful canvas,
Just let me give in all that I have for you.
Oh! but it will take the next few lives too, since
Sky's the limit of my love for you, therefore
One lifetime isn't enough for me to let you know,
How precious you are to my soul.
Just let me
Show you the world through my eyes,
And all you'll see is *you*.
Just let me
Help you feel alive after being breathless
for most of your life.
Just let me give in all that I have for you,
My dearest,
I don't want you to do
anything for me,
I just want you to let me do
everything for you,
Just let me.

Tanishka Tyagi

One Soul

I'm scared,
What if
You don't feel like how you felt from afar,
What if
You're different than what I saw from afar,
Just like the Moon
That seems pretty from the land
But in the sky, it is all alone, lonely, dark
And has a hollow soul.
But that's what love is
I believe,
You've always shown me the real you,
And so no matter what
I will always be with you,
I will always love you for who you are,
I will always support you,
I will fill your soul with love.

Tanishka Tyagi

One Soul

Did you know?
Your soul is better than heaven.
You must know,
Your soul is better than heaven.
Therefore, when I die,
I'd rather want to live in your soul
Than leading to heaven.

One Soul

Oh! you're the one who gives me
The warmth of your love in these cold days,
Oh! you're the rain
On my hottest humid days,
Oh! you are the cool breeze
Blowing around me,
Oh! you are the one to
Make my soul feel at ease.
You're everything lovely,
Everything beautiful,
Everything that makes my life, a life.
You're everything that makes me want to live,
You're literally life in itself.

I think I love you a little way too much,
So much that the pupils of your eyes
Seems like the moon to me,
So much the smile of your heart
Seems like the universe to me,
So much that your soul
Feels like home to me,
So much that, this healing voice of yours,
Seems like heartbeat to me,
So much that you
You, my love, you
Seem like life to me.

~ I am glad you're you,
You make me want to be myself too,
Thank you for being you,
Since I can be "me" too, with you.

Tanishka Tyagi

One Soul

Isn't it fascinating,
How I have no idea of how you feel in real,
But there's you in my mind,
That makes me feel so alive,
I know the day I see you,
I would be blind
For the rest of the world.

Isn't it fascinating,
How I've never heard
Your voice calling my name,
But there's a you in my mind,
Singing a song written through
The words of my love,
I know the day I hear you call my name,
I'd be deaf
For the rest of the world.

Isn't it fascinating,
How we're not together right now
Yet forever always,
I promise even if we become
Two completely different stars
In the universe,
We will unite one day,
And make our own Galaxy,
Just you and me,
So tell me, isn't it fascinating?

Tanishka Tyagi

One Soul

The time keeps flying,
It scares me and excites me
At the same time,
How gloomy to have felt,
I am growing each second,
So depressing it is to see
each second just pass by.

The moments we've spent together
Will soon be gone forever,
What they'll leave behind are
The memories that will
Be cherished forever.

The life you gave me
Has to end someday,
Ohh! how it hurts
To even think that way,
But let's go back to the days
When we learnt to live,
To breathe and to smile,
When all we did was to stay
Young, free and wild,
Doing what are souls heard,
And what our hearts felt,
Ohh! how bad I wish
I could turn back time.

I don't know
What the sky holds
For us in the future,
I just hope it's sunshine,
And not the rain.
I've spent quite a while
In monsoon,
Now hey time?

Tanishka Tyagi

One Soul

Can you please take
Us to the spring noon?

let's live, let's just live
From the beginning,
Without thinking about how
The time flies,
But promise me
Even when the time comes
For our separation,
You and me will be
Like the fragrance of rose,
Let's not leave each other
Until we leave ourselves.

But in the end,
Time will never stop flying,
But that must not stop us
From spreading our wings,
We shall fly too,
We shall live too,

All of this time will be memories soon.

Tanishka Tyagi

One Soul

Even though
You're away from me,
You're the only one
I have with me.

Tanishka Tyagi

6:13pm

*Even though
You're away from me
You're the only one
I have with me*

One Soul

Until I breath,
My soul belong to yours.
Until I live,
My eyes will look for yours.
It's an eternal thing,
I'll never remorse.
Even if you can never be mine,
I'll always be yours.
For love isn't a barter system,
A selfless love, is a love meant to be.
And with that,
I promise
To ask for nothing
In requite of the feeling
Of loving you,
The feeling that comes from
Being in love with you,
Is in Itself something that gives me
A reason to smile,
A will to shine,
The eyes that speak,
Emotions that rhyme,
And a life to live,
With utmost tranquility.

~My soul will always be engraved
With your soul's name.

Tanishka Tyagi

One Soul

For once,
I wish you be the Sun &
not the Moon,
Not the Moon who's presence is questioned
In the noon.
Rather, I wish for once,
You be the Sun,
Who lights the one,
That lights the night.

For since,
You're my Sun,
I am your Moon,
You're the source of my light,
The reason why I shine,
The one that makes me bright.
If you weren't there
I would have been just a dark,
Depressed, hollow soul
With circular emotions of
Sadness that has no end.
But now that I have you,
I have my self.
You give me life,
You give me light.
You're my Sun,
I am your Moon,
You're the source of my life.

Tanishka Tyagi

One Soul

I am not afraid of death,
What fears me is
The feeling of falling apart,
Falling apart from my soul,
Falling apart from you.
But the fear will fear itself,
The day
You'll let me live
in your soul.

~ The death will be afraid
To fall us apart.

One Soul

How was your day?
Tell me how was your day?
Isn't it something you've
Always wanted to be asked about?
I know you've always wanted to be asked about
The smallest yet the most precious
Thing that we do? Right?
I'm here. I'm always here.
Don't shy away! Tell me how was your day?
Come, let's sit together by the riverside,
Let's hold hands gently and
Talk about everything that you wish to.
Sometimes questions like these are the ones
That makes us feel alive.

"How was your day?
Did you eat?
Did you smile?
Did you get happy?"
I will be the one
To ask you what no one does.
I will be your friend,
Your perpetual listener,
And your eternal lover
As long as I'm here,
You needn't worry over
Who's going to take care of you.
As long as I am here,
I'll make sure, you have yourself.

Tanishka Tyagi

One Soul

You've seen the world,
And I've seen you.
My eyes saw the rarest scenery
You get to see only when
Your eyes meet the mirror's.
Hence, I've got a better view ,
Rather I've got the best view.
Better than the world,
Better than the world's,
The best ever.

Tanishka Tyagi

One Soul

I wonder why the world is so mean,
I wonder how they stay happy by making others teary.
I wonder what makes them so envious of me?
I try to make myself not care about anything,
Just by looking at you, I feel healed.
You protect me like the ozone layer,
You whisper into my soul that "I mustn't care,"
I wonder, you're literally a sunrise , a sunshine,
A ray of hope, a ray of life.
Making my soul at ease
when I feel like being on high rise,
Just by looking at you,
I know what makes them so envious of me.
And I don't wonder anymore,
I wander.

One Soul

My heart aches.
At times I really wish to scream to the world
The amount of love I have for you,
If only the world considers it,
Love and not obsession,
Longing and not greed,
Purity and not loss of sanity,
If only they'll ever understand ~
And if only I'll ever be able
To make them understand…

~ For our love isn't meant
To be understood,
It is to be felt.
So I decide to keep quiet
And scream in silence.

Tanishka Tyagi

One Soul

I see you in the sky,
Around me every time,
In the day; you shine,
At night; you light,
You just never disappear,
Giving me hopes in
Despair.

It's the way we talk to each other,
Through the universe.
Always know you've got me,
Even at your worst.
Although I am miles away,
I'll be there when u call my name.

Tanishka Tyagi

One Soul

I will always choose you,
I will always choose to
live with a thought of you
than to live with
the feeling of being with someone
Who's not you,
Than to love someone
Who's not you.

Huh?
Are there many souls in a body?
No. Right? And never will be.
There's only one soul,
And always will be.
my soul is you.
Since ever & evermore .
Hence, A thought of you
To me, Is a hope of life.

Thusly, I will always choose you,
I will always choose to
live with a thought of you,
If not you.

Tanishka Tyagi

One Soul

At times,
When I ask myself "Why do I love you so much ?"
I don't have any reasons as such…
Or say the reasons I have for loving you,
Pale in comparison to why I love you.
And I think that's why I love you,
I think that's what true love is.
You're you and that's enough,
For me to be in love with you.

You don't need reasons to be loved,
For the reasons might change with time,
But my love will never, my love is
Immutably everlasting, hence
You, my love,
You are all my reasons
For why I love you.
For I believe, there's only you,
That won't change
Even with time.
Hence,
You, my love,
You are all my reasons
For why I love you.
And I think this is
What true love is.

Tanishka Tyagi

A LIST OF REASONS
I LOVE YOU
===

1. YOU'RE YOU.

One Soul

Wish I could call the Moon "mine,"
Wish I could walkthrough
The riverside with
The Moon at night,
Wish I could listen
To songs with
The Moon in peace,
Wish I could talk to
The Moon all the time,
Wish I could watch
The Moon straight in his eyes.

Wish you were here,
With me by my side.

Notes

One Soul

Definition of *me:*
A person who loves you beyond forever.

10:13 pm

"Definition of me
 ___ you"

One Soul

Somewhere in the parallel universe,
We're both together.
Trust me. Trust me,
This is the parallel universe
I am talking about.
With this, I promise you,
We'll be together,
Trust me.
It might take a while,
But not the whole of our time.
Just, trust me.

Cause Even though,
My hands are dying
To feel a touch of you,
My eyes are craving
To see a glimpse of you,
Nevertheless,
I am glad my soul is trying
To make it all happen,
To be with you.

It's tough but not impossible,
I'll make "you and me" to "we,"
Oh ! Just trust me,
I will never let anything
Come in my way
From you and me to we,
It's tough but not impossible.
It might take a while,
But not the whole of our time.
All we need is a little bit of faith.

Tanishka Tyagi

My soul was made to love yours.

One Soul

Romeo and Juliet?
Sure we do love it,
But did we ever give a thought to
Neil Armstrong and the Moon.
This one's kinda special,
So I let this breath forever
In the pages of "soul."

~ Remember, how
The Moon was afar from Neil,
But he did never kneel.
Likewise, here in our story
The Moon is you
And I have a hue
That I will be with you,
And I'll make you feel
That you're not so far,
You're not so away,
You're not so alone
And not so left out.

So when I meet you,
I'll tell you every story,
Every time a person said
I can't have you,
They knew you were my Moon,
But in a way that
I will never reach out to you,
In a way that you're too far away,
But you are and always will be
My Moon in the way,
You make me feel so whole,
How you are my only light,
How love is all about you in my life,
And so I decided
To become an astronaut,

Tanishka Tyagi

One Soul

Come to you no matter what,
No matter how many years it might take,
And tell them, tell everyone
That nothing was ever impossible,
If believed.
So when I meet you,
I'll tell you every story,
Stories where,
The astronaut was me,
The Moon was always you.

Tanishka Tyagi

One Soul

The love in my eye,
The pride in my heart,
The longing in my soul,
The more and more I fall,
It's never ending,
It keeps me going,
The love in my veins,
The warmth in my hug,
The comfort in my voice,
The home in my soul,
It's never ending,
It keeps increasing,
It's all for you
The way I long,
The way I love.
It's only for you.
The way I long,
The way I love.

Tanishka Tyagi

One Soul

I had so much for you,
I started expressing it
through poems,
But as I write more & more
I realize I have so much more for you,
To put into words.
I realized that even if
I write a million poems,
worth a boundless emotions,
and a trillion words filled with love,
I'll still have so much more
For you, to put into words.

One Soul

And if ever you ask me,
"How are you so sure
About no one being able to
Love me as much as you?"
I'll tell you,
I wasn't, I was never sure of it
However I became,
Became very sure of it,
I became so sure
About no one being able to love you
As much I do
When I felt you breathing in my soul,
When I felt each breath of yours, in my soul,
I realized how I was living only for you,
How I am living only cause of you.

They say,"You live for yourself."
So if someone else does it,
You know you're in their soul
Perhaps, you're they're soul.
And they're so into you,
They start to live for you
For the rest of their life.
They start to see you in themselves ,
Like I always do.
You have captivated my soul
With yours, my beloved.
I've no words to ever
Tell you, how I am
So sure.

Tanishka Tyagi

One Soul

Let's show them a story like ours,
Loving each other like
The Moon love the stars.

Tanishka Tyagi

One Soul

I've felt the you,
You hid in your soul.
I've seen the you,
You're too scared to show.
I've loved the you,
You didn't show to the world.
Darling, when I say,
I love you,
I mean the you,
Perhaps even you don't know.
Just how we've never seen ourselves,
In the absence of mirrors & lens.
And You know, we never can.
Thusly Make me your mirror and see yourself
Through my eyes , for once my love.
You'll be in love with yourself too,
I am not to be blamed, there's just something
So sacred about you.
Ah! You know what I mean.
You just have to know,
Thus perhaps,
I am the lens to your soul,
And at times, I see
Even things you don't show.

~ I love the inner child in you ,
No one ever asked about.

Tanishka Tyagi

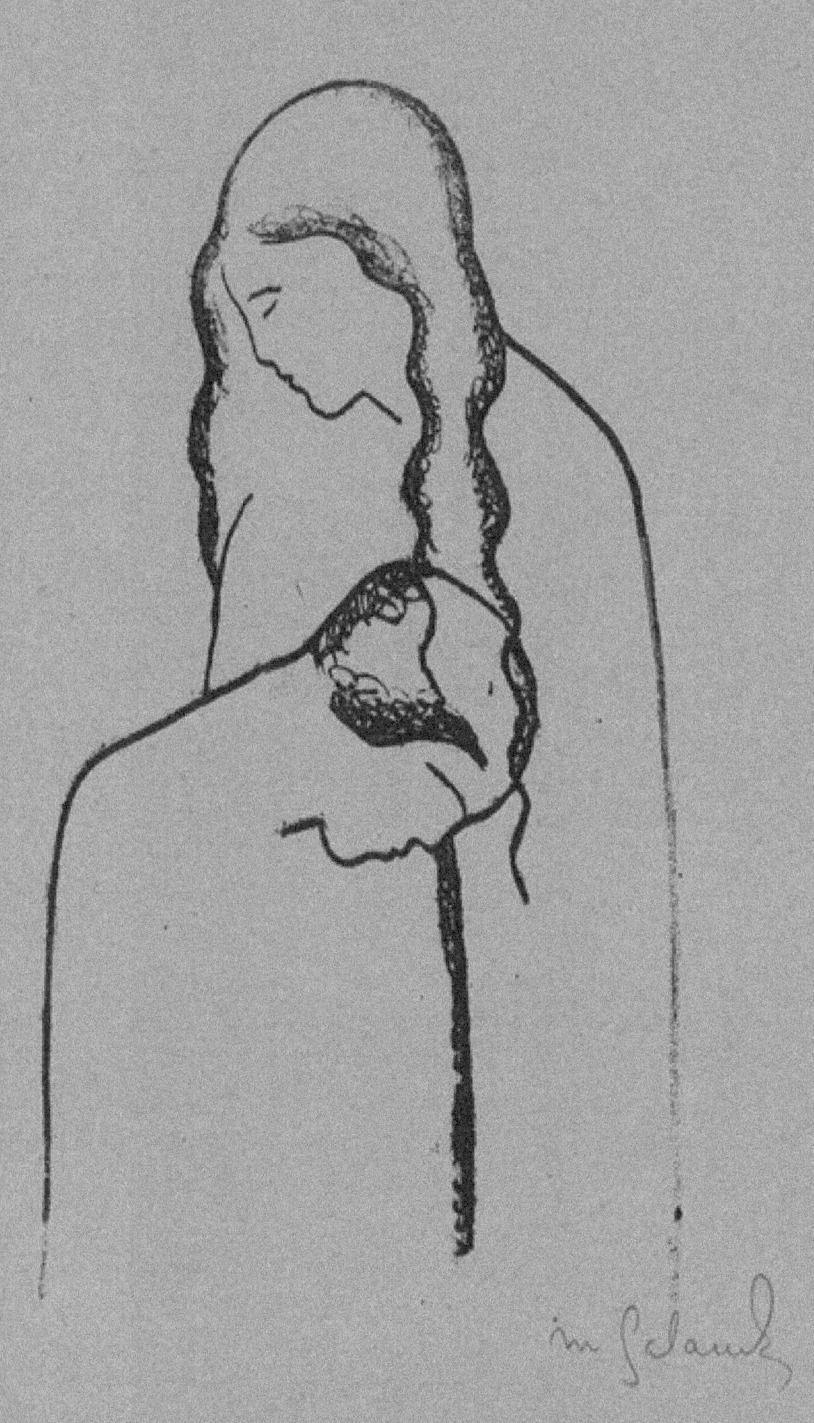

One Soul

And if my heart was asked to be torn,
They'll see every piece of it
Engraved with your name.

One Soul

You're just a little far,
Not apart,
And never will be.
I will find my way to you,
In this and every lifetime
That we'll be in.
Remember,
Just a little afar,
Not apart,
And never will be.
I will find my way to you,
In this and every lifetime
That will be.

One Soul

I wonder,
What you would've been to me
If I wasn't a human?
Like, if I was a flower,
Would you be my spring?
You'd be the spring.
If I was a bumblebee,
You'd be my lavender.
If I was a cloud,
You'd be the sky.
If I was a river,
You'd be the ocean.
If I was the Moon,
You'd be my Sun.
If I was an Art,
Would you be my Museum?
since a museum without art,
Would be nothing but four walls,
And for the art without museum,
Would never be preserved and
Acknowledged extensively,
Perhaps museum and art without each other,
Might always just be a matter of vision,
Unaware of the impact of creation and imagination.
Thusly , You'd be my museum.
However, since I am a human
With a body and mind,
You'd be my soul,
For this life.

Tanishka Tyagi

One Soul

You're like a candle,
That lights up the room in the dark
When no one's around,
You put your soul on fire
To light up the world,
So selflessly,
Melting, yet lightening.
~ I could never be grateful enough to you
For being the light in my somber life.

Tanishka Tyagi

One Soul

My love, I hope you don't expect
Anything from anyone, in life.
Expectations hurt, they bury you alive.
and I would rather want to die
than to see you cry.
I hope all you get is happiness,
For you deserve the brightest smile.
I hope all you feel is love,
For you deserve to experience
The most beautiful part of being alive.
I……
I hope you never feel alone
For you are not alone, never alone.
I am always with you
Even if you can't see me
I hope you feel me
I hope I can be like the sky to you,
A little too far, I am sorry
But always with you.
I hope I can be like the sky to you,
So You can always look up to me,
When needed.
So you can always feel my presence,
Even in your solitude.
So you can always feel my essence
The essence of my love,
The essence of my warmth.
You're never alone
I am always with you, my love.

Tanishka Tyagi

One Soul

The home was always a place
Until I met you,
Now it's a soul.
My home is a soul,
A person, an emotion,
It's you.
You're my home.

Tanishka Tyagi

One Soul

I took birth,
But only existed on Earth
Until I met you, and
Now that I've met you
It feels like a rebirth
But to be alive, this time.

11:00pm

"Ever since I met you I felt how dead I was all along until I met you

One Soul

I like to imagine,
I like to visualize my life with you,
Every second of it , every moment of it ,
Every ounce of my life being with you.
So for once, please listen up!
Something I've thought for us in my mind ,
Such I promise, soon will come to life.

—My love and me, you and me,
We go to a museum,
We're in thoughts of amaze,
It feels surreal,
"This is all I've ever wanted!!"

With you, you my art,
To go see arts!
Now here we are, at the museum,
I see you admiring the art,
While I admire the art
No artist could ever paint,
Merely your parents,
That being you.
I look at you for as long as I could,
Woefully! with only "two" eyes,
For how long can I look?
The best will be,
The rest of my life.

You knew I was looking at you,
And so you looked at the art more passionately,
It was time to move ahead, when suddenly
You say "Wait lemme take a picture of you,"
So now you could admire me too,
The grids of the camera are all focused on me…
And the art you claimed "Beautiful",
Became a blurred hue.

Tanishka Tyagi

One Soul

Oh! we're so in love, we both know!
But how beautifully do we act as if we don't.
A love like this is meant to last for an eternity.

I can't seem to look at the art,
When I do, in the end it's always you,
Nothing seems prettier than now,
"Now" where you're here with me.

Next we go to an off grid cottage
In an English land,
A place with nothing
but moments of love being spent,
With you, being here , life seems as if
I am living in Watson's "Ode to Vivian."

It was all bright, but
Suddenly the skies turn black,
I guess the god has some other plans,
His's are better than mine, so nevermind.
The rain has started pouring,
Look love, me and you made the clouds cry.
The union even the sky's been longing,
Not just you and I ,
And now I am not the only one falling.

An English land in rain,
No less than a dream, with you.
We can't miss frolicking here,
So we move to the backyard;
Wooden fence, green meadow,
And a white horse that won't harm.
He's wondering that if he was a human,
He too would want a love story like ours.
Admiration in everyone's eye, the nature,
The animal and the god's sight.

Tanishka Tyagi

One Soul

You seem so happy, hence so am I.
Since we both love the rain,
Running, playing along,
Endeavors to clench each other,
So just for once, we could have it all,
You in my arm , and me in yours.
And when we do,
Please don't let me go,
Please don't let me go at all.
You, keep me in your arms &
We gently fall once again,
In a land we're made for,
The land of love peace & art.
This time the love being for
An eternity and beyond.

Now the rain stops pouring,
The sky seems clear with stars and Moon,
We look at the them
While you pull me closer to you.
I can hear your heart beat,
while mine's holding me.
Now as we look at them,
They look at us too,
Little do we know,
even the stars and the Moon
Are admiring me and you.

Now we get inside the cottage ,
It's chilling outside but we loved every second,
So we're here to capture these moments
In a book of love and soul through ink.

Tanishka Tyagi

One Soul

Picking up a pen ,
on our way to write what we just felt,
But oh! the issue is ,
I can write the whole song,
Except for the chorus,
That only you can form.
I know you could do that really well !
So now I hand over my incomplete song into your hands ,
We've now immortalized the moments we spent.
You write me a chorus and it's a whole again.
The incomplete song, felt complete again.

Since to my every song,
You've been the chorus of all.
My darling, to even "The song of my soul."

Tanishka Tyagi

One Soul

I'd die for you?
I'd live for you.

You like books?
I'll write for you.

I'll write a thousand books for you,
I'll write a thousand books on you ,
If only they will ever be enough to
Express my love for you.

I am not good at singing,
But I'd sing for you.
I can't dance like you do,
But I'd dance with you,
I'd dance with you
If that makes you happy,
Under the moonlight,
On a rainy day, in the snow,
I'd dance with you, whenever you feel low.
I can't keep myself quiet
Even for a while, I love to speak !!!!!
But trust me,
I'd listen to you
For the rest of my life, only you.
Being quiet and just living in the
Melodious voice of your soul,
Could there be anything better than
A feeling of breathing in the same air as you?

~ I can't make quick decisions,
It's tough for me to choose between two,
I seem to be kinda indecisive,
But look I just made the best decision,
Of being in love with you.

Tanishka Tyagi

A soul like yours is worth loving.

One Soul

Even when I die,
My love will always remain in this book,
Breathing the air of your love.
Even when I die,
You will always be alive in me,
In the form of my soul,
For the body perhaps buried,
The soul is everlasting ,
For my soul is all yours,
And you are all in my soul.
Hence, even when I die,
My love will always remain in this book,
Breathing the air of your love.

Tanishka Tyagi

One Soul

When you *think* like you're in love,
There comes a conception in your mind,
Of the world being unaware of you,
Except that one person,
And thus, you dislike most of the world except
That one person.
But when you *fall* in love,
You love the world because
Of that one person,
Because of the way
They make it so beautiful to you.
The way they change
Your complete vision of life,
You just love it so much,
It comes to you,
It just comes to you subliminally,
You fall in love
With the concept of life.
That is when you know,
You fell in love.
And not with the *thought* of
Falling in love.

~ This is what I realized,
When I looked into those eyes of yours.

Tanishka Tyagi

One Soul

I've reached the level of love,
Where keeping silence
Seems like the loudest way
Of expressing my love,
For you.
And where writing
Seems like the most heard way
Of confessing my love,
For you.

Tanishka Tyagi

One Soul

They say,
"One should not love anyone
More than themselves,"
Oh! but you?
You're so well dwelled in me
That I'll love you eternally,
Either way.

you were the missing piece. my heart was made for you all along.

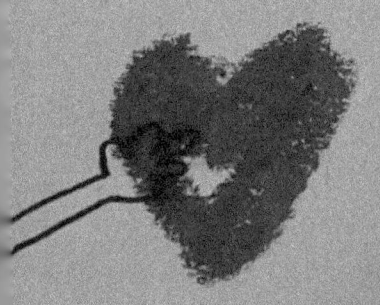

One Soul

When my time comes,
Even if you aspire to,
Don't look at me in my
Eyes.
For, I will not be able to
Die.

One Soul

And one day, I realized,
Suddenly all of the love songs
Got me thinking of you.
Suddenly all of the lovely things
Reminded me of you.
Suddenly all the beautiful soulful words
Were about you, for you and to you.
Suddenly all my mind did
Was to think of you,
Suddenly when I said I love you,
It meant only for you.
It was all sudden but
Hereafter, it's meant to be eternal.

One Soul

Someone asked me,
"What is love?"
I said ;
If I told you,
If I described it,
If I could mould
An eternal emotion like
Love into words,
Then *WHAT IS LOVE?*

~ However, isn't it astonishing?
How there's one word and only one word
That's even greater than love,
You.

One Soul

I wish to paint my poems
On the canvas of your soul.

One Soul

My love,
Your eyes aren't just something
I wanna look in,
You have the Galaxy,
I wanna be a star in.

One Soul

And while the pages of my soul
Come to an end,
I realized how I wish this would
Never end, idealistically possible,
Perhaps not practically.
Hence, I'd want to remind you
That I will always love you.
And only you more than ever,
More than forever.
More than you can think,
And can ever wonder.
More than you've ever felt,
And will ever ponder.
I will love you beyond forever.

Tanishka Tyagi

Notes

One Soul

The time passes,
And with each second,
I love you more.
The Sun keeps shining,
And with each ray of light,
I love you more.
The flowers keep blooming,
And with each bud,
I love you more.
The ocean keeps moving,
And with each wave that
Hits the shore,
I love you more.
The rain keeps pouring,
And with each drop,
I love you more.

Tanishka Tyagi

11:11 am

*The time passes
And with each second
I love you more*

One Soul

"How do you know he's 'the one' ?"

Oh! I am an ocean wanderer,
So I look straight into his eyes,
And I realize,
He's not only 'the one',
But also the 'only one'.

~ *His eyes are the ocean.*

One Soul

So that you don't take my words as
Just a poem,
I'll say it again to reassure ,
I will listen to you,
Your eyes,
Your emotions,
Your actions,
Your soul,
Each breath of yours,
They speak,
They howl in love quietly,
And I am here to listen,
Alive or dead,
With my ears next to your lips,
I am here to listen.
I will listen to all your stories.
I will ask you "How are you?"
I will ask you "If you've been happy?"
I will listen like a thalassophile
Listening to the voice of the waves,
I will be your *soul's forever listener.*

Tanishka Tyagi

talk.
i'll listen.

One Soul

If only there was anything
More valuable than your smile,
I would count the stars.
If only there was anything
More precious than your words,
I would touch the sky.
If only there was anything
Purer than your soul,
I would guzzle the ocean.

~To be who you are,
Is impossible.

To be who you are
Is impossible

One Soul

They said,
"One day I'll stop falling for you,"
I said eventually even the universe
Will come to an end.
So where lies my love?
Beyond the universe?
Within the universe?
O my love,
They didn't know
My love for you is
In itself a universe,
Our universe.
And our universe is meant
To live for an infinity,
And beyond.

Tanishka Tyagi

One Soul

Oh! how hard it is,
To stay away from the one
That makes you want to stay.

~ Oh! how hard it is for me
To stay away from you.

One Soul

If I could, I would,
I would take away all your troubles,
And give you a life with no hurdle,
But would that be worth living?
In a life with no hurdles ,
Would you ever get a chance
To be proud of who you are?
And who you've become?
Would you ever realize
How strong you are ?

If I could I would,
I would take away all your sadness,
And give you days filled with joy & happiness,
But would that ever make you realize
How precious, your smile is ?
Would you ever feel the feeling of being happy
When all you'd do is be happy?

It's the days we've got,
We must savour.
It's the life we've got,
We must live.
We'll get old,
But we must stay young
Eternally, internally, mentally.
We'll have downs ,
But we have a soul of a lover,
To be able to do anything,
Is no big deal for us.
Me & you, we,
We'll have days of gloom,
Yet in the fullness of time,
Let's bear in mind to bloom.

Tanishka Tyagi

One Soul

So darling,
The next time it rains,
Let's not be hopeless
And wait until the Sun shine.
Just so we can be grateful
For the sunrise,
After a week of overcast sky.

One Soul

My beloved,
To die in your eyes;
The most peaceful end to my life.
And being buried in your soul
Will be the *most alive grave of my life.*

One Soul

I hope all those times I've spent
Looking at the Moon wondering if
You are looking too,
You were looking too.

You were looking too, hoping
That someone must be looking too,
And I was looking too,
Wondering that you'd be looking too.

I hope all those times I've spent
Looking at the Moon wondering if
You are looking too,
You were looking too.

You were looking too, hoping
That someone must be looking too,
And I was looking too,
Wondering that you'd be looking too.

That's how the two of us always
Stayed connected through the Moon.
Wondering and wandering about the Moon.

i told the moon

to watch over
you

One Soul

I know it's a cliche',
But what if I tell you "you're my everything."

Everything in a way that,
When I look at the flowers, I think of you.
When I listen to love songs, I think of you.
When I watch the Moon , I think of you.
When I smell lavender , I think of you.
When I write poetries , I think of you.

And so I do,
When it rains,
When it snows,
When spring arrives,
When the sky speaks,
And the beings stay quiet
When it's all dark and just
The stars shine.

Everything in a way that ,
When I paint, it's always your eyes.
when I dream, it's always you and me.
When I eat, I think of if you've had your meal?
When I write, it's always for you.
When I think, it's always of you.
When I speak, it's always about you.

I know it's a cliché ,
But trust me when I say,
"You're my everything,"
I mean everything in a way ,
That goes beyond everything.

Tanishka Tyagi

One Soul

From the core of my heart,
Even though we've never felt
The feeling of being together, yet…

Despite that, I can feel your presence,
And unfortunately also your absence…

In your absence ,
Something about me remains obscure,
Something in my soul remains exotic,
A place in my heart remains untrodden,
Finds out it's none howbeit *"you"*.

In your absent presence
I can feel how your presence feel,
When all I've ever felt is a glance of you,
Through the stars and the sky.
I can feel my heart ache for a glimpse of you,
Exactly how the universe feels
When a star becomes a meteor,
Breaking shattering and falling apart
In pieces as a whole in universe.
Exactly how the Pluto felt,
When it couldn't be a planet and
Had to stay forever as a dwarf.

When you're not here,
My soul feels like kīlauea volcano,
Lava explodes within me,
Making every ounce of my soul burn.
Oh ! But with you,
Thou, my ocean,
Within you stashes my soul's serenity,
You make me calm,
It's in your presence that the volcano within me
Subsides with a drop of your soul's tranquility.

One Soul

And the lost stars in me
That once became a meteor,
Seem to shine brighter than ever,
as a whole in my soul.
O my universe !
Please come home, come to me.
Now, I've been waiting for you ,
For quite a long, soulfully.

Tanishka Tyagi

10:01 pm

It's in your presence that the volcano within me subsides with a drop of your soul's tranquility

One Soul

My love, lookup,
Look up and have a glance at yourself
In the sky,
In the solar system,
Do you see yourself?
Cause I see you.
Every time I see the solar system,
I see you.
You're immense,
And considerably enormous
Than the universe.
You possess the universe
Within you.
You possess the power of stars
Within you.
Why would I look up
At the universe,
When I've got you,
Oh! but you, look up,
Look up and have a glance of
The solar system in the sky,
Have a glance at you,
Do you see yourself?
Cause I see you.

Tanishka Tyagi

One Soul

I can't sleep when
I think of you,
I don't want to sleep while
I think of you,
The emptiness of falling asleep,
Forsaking *your* thoughts in amidst,
I can't do this,
Perhaps I don't want to do this.
Rather I'd just think of you,
And stay awake from dusk till dawn,
All night long.
Thoughts of you are more serene,
So when I say
Thoughts of you keep me awake,
I mean it saves me
From the sleep of life,
From the desolation
And miseries of life ,
From the land of woe,
Often disguised as land of nod,
From the placid turbulent,
World of dysphoria.
And so I can't sleep when
I think of you,
I don't want to sleep while
I think of you.
The emptiness of falling asleep,
Forsaking *your* thoughts in amidst,
I can't do this,
Perhaps I don't want to do this.

—*Written at midnight*—

Tanishka Tyagi

One Soul

"*La vie, c'est des étapes*
la plus douce, c'est l'amour
la plus dure, c'est la separation
la plus pénible, c'est les adieux
la plus belle, c'est les retrouvailes"

French anonymous quote

"Life is stages:
The sweetest is love,
The hardest is separation,
The most painful is goodbye,
The most beautiful is *reunion*."

One Soul

Its crazy How,
I think of you
And have tears in my eyes.
For there's so much,
Nothing else could ever describe.

Tears are the unspoken words,
The non vocable emotions.
Tears aren't just a drop of water,
They're a drop of my soul.
An incomprehensible feeling,
A form of love so divinely pure.
Tears are the words of one's soul.

So when I think of you,
Looking at how you're as soft
As a feather,
As Divine as a seraphic treasure,
I have tears in my eyes.
For there are no words
To describe what I feel
When I look into your eyes.

One Soul

I hope you know,
Your soul is comprised of
All the celestial bodies that has
Ever existed and will ever exist.

Tanishka Tyagi

One Soul

As much as I love the sea,
I fear the sea.
I fear losing myself
Consciousness and drowning,
I fear myself getting lost and,
Never coming back again.
But that's love,
That's how it's always supposed to be.
It scares you and excites you
At the same time,
Love makes you feel lost
In the most cognizant manner.
Love makes you feel stood
Despite of have fallen,
Love is nothing but a metaphor of life,
So with that,
I love the sea.
You're my sea,
I want to drown in your soul.
Drown in the most lively manner,
Since, *that's love.*

Tanishka Tyagi

One Soul

I hope you live for
Eternity and beyond.
I hope your soul be
Free and wild until the
The universe breathes.
I hope you smile till
The last star in the galaxy
Breaks into an oblivion.
I hope you shine until
The Sun shines in the solar system.
I hope I can love you
The way you wish to be loved.
I hope, to you I can be,
What *you* are to me.
I hope and hope and hope
Until the hope dies.
Hence, I hope and hope and hope
Until my soul dies.

Tanishka Tyagi

10:01 pm

I hope you smile
till
The last star in
the galaxy
Breaks into an
oblivion

One Soul

I long for you
To come home soon,
For my soul longs for you,
Every Moon.

One day, soon
Under the same moon,
We'll be *one soul,*
Feeling like a whole,
Feeling like we've never felt before,
Feeling like this is all we need at all,
Feeling like this is what we were meant for.
One day, soon
Under the same Moon,
We'll be *one soul.*

~ I'll be waiting until you come home.
Home, the place I built out of my soul,
The place your love built in my soul,
Home, the place you and I have made ,
For one another,
In our souls.

I built you a
home in my heart

One Soul

So, today let's live in the future,
Let's live in the moment of our union,
Let's breathe the same feeling,
Let's surround us with the same emotion,
Let's just drown in each other's soul
While we watch the Moon lying on the floor,
Let's just live in one another's world,
Let me be you and let yourself be mine.
Let's just create what we've always dreamt of,
Something vividly reminiscent of love.
Let me love your every flaw and perfection,
Let's create a forever, together,
Let's promise to perish together,
For, I won't ever leave you alone,
And I don't wish to be left with no soul.
So, today
Let's live in the future,
Let's live in the moment of our union,
Let's breathe the same feeling,
Let's surround us with the same emotions.

Tanishka Tyagi

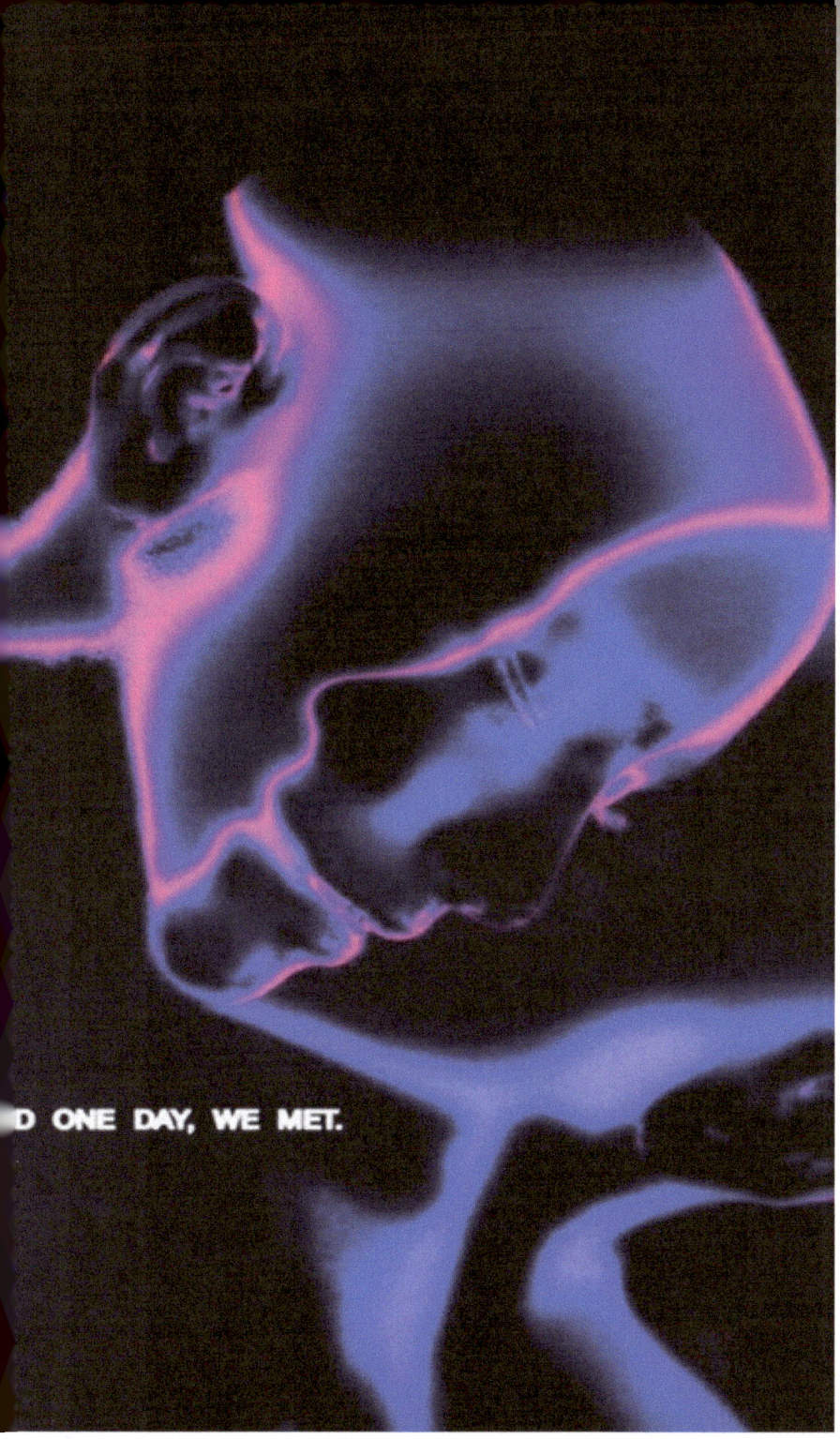

One Soul

Hey! You've reached till here,
I assume you've read all those things above,
There's so much about the Moon,
And the stars and the galaxy and the universe.
I used them to define you.
I don't feel like there's anything else
That can define you,
Though, even the cosmos isn't everything
That defines you perfectly ,
There's so much more, that I see in you.
But believe me,
There's something about the universe,
Every time it reminds me of you.
However, I hope you don't take them
As just words that rhyme,
Or words that were written to make a poem.
I sincerely hope,
You consider my words and
Look into you soul once again,
To seek for the universe I see in you,
Which for you, is still untrodden.

Tanishka Tyagi

10:13pm

*Even the cosmos
isn't everything
That defines you
perfectly
There's so much
more that I see
in you*

My love

One Soul

Do you know how I love you?
I'll tell you...
I want to make you smile,
Make you laugh,
Make your eyes shine,
I want to give you the love you deserve,
I want to give you the love of the universe,
I want to do the simplest yet
Most beautiful things for you,
I want to make you hot chocolate,
I want to buy you rings and flowers,
I want to give you gifts,
I want to make you handmade cards.
I want to write you love letters,
I want to get your name tattooed on my soul,
I want to .... do everything,
Not just be with you when you're happy,
I want to be with you on your gloomy days.
I want to make you smile,
Make you laugh,
Make your eyes shine.

Do you know how I want *our* love to be?
I'll tell you...
I want it as simple as *breathing air,*
I want us to watch the "The Notebook" together
While we lay on the couch,
I want us to walk by the river side together
Holding hands and giggling around,
I want us to listen to love songs
While the lights of the room fall asleep,
I want us to sit back and look at the stars
Then look into each other's eyes,
I want us to go on top of the hill,
Sit on the grass and be pleased
By the city view at midnight,

Tanishka Tyagi

Vue du Staubbach
à Lauterbrunen.

One Soul

I want us to go to the beach at 3:00 am,
When no one's around,
just me, you and the Moonlight.
I want us to visit museums
And see each other in the art.
I want us to confess love
Besides the Lauterbrunnen Fall,
I want us to write poems,
Lyrics, paint canvas, sing songs,
I want us to just be free
And be what we want to be.
I want us to be immortalized in arts,
Just as in my poems.
I just….
I just want us
To be in each other's soul,
All I want is you and me,
Me and you !
My dear universe, is that a little too-
I want us to pour our hearts out to each other,
I want us to love like the old school lovers.
I really want us,
I really want us to be *one soul.*

The words did not
Justify my emotions,
I really want our love
As deep as the ocean.

I want so much more,
I'll always be wanting more,
With you.
With you,
I need the whole of you.

Tanishka Tyagi

One Soul

I hope now
You have an idea of how
I want to love you,
Exactly how an artist loves it's muse.

One Soul

For the readers : (from the author)

Life ? What is life ?
Life is all about..
Falling in love with music,
Wandering lost in art.
Life is all about..
Celebrating the little things,
Finding peace in nature.
Life is all about..
Being in the universe,
Being in love with the universe.
Fetish for flowers and four leaf clover,
Life is all about..
Capturing the golden hour,
Playing chords on guitar.
Life ? It's ease.
Trust me and live it, for once.
You'll love it.
Life is all about..
Spending time with one's soul,
Painting canvas in a cottage
Beside the Swiss mounts.
Life is all about…
Loving,
Loving art ,
Loving oneself,
Loving the expansive nature,
Loving the universe,
And love is all in you.
Hence, Life is within you,
Trust me and live it, for once.
You'll love it.

Tanishka Tyagi

One Soul

Life is easy,
It's all about loving.
Maybe that's why,
It seems difficile.
However, since it's about loving,
I love it, I love loving.
I hope you can too,
Lively love life.

Tanishka Tyagi

One Soul

O My beloved !
Look what you
Did to me,
Made my soul a
Writer, subliminally
*Now this shall be
Continued….
For an eternity.*

Tanishka Tyagi

www.ingramcontent.com/pod-product-compliance
Lightning Source LLC
LaVergne TN
LVHW061629070526
838199LV00071B/6629